POCKET
PARABLES

POCKET PARABLES

CARL G. CARLOZZI

Tyndale House
Publishers, Inc.
Wheaton, Illinois

I wish to express my very special thanks to: the Reverend Douglas C. Smith, my senior associate, for his creative input and patience on those days when I drove him to distraction reading parables to him; Paul Meyer for his input relating to the brokerage business; L. Gene Lemon and Armen Ervanian for their input relating to corporate structure and business practices; Robert T. Murphy and William W. Clements for input relating to legal matters; and to all the people of All Saints' Parish who live the gospel of compassion, kindness, and forgiveness in their lives.

All Scripture is taken from the Revised Standard Version.

First printing, June 1985
Library of Congress Catalog Card Number 84-52610
ISBN 0-8423-4919-7
Copyright 1985 by Carl G. Carlozzi
All rights reserved
Printed in the United States of America

Dedicated
to
Dr. Robert Schuller,
whose ministry is
a powerful example
of what the
kingdom of God
is like.

What is all this talk about virgins and their lamps, savorless salt, tares, mustard seeds, wineskins, motes and beams, unjust stewards, and a whole host of other things with which I am totally unfamiliar? What in the world is Jesus talking about? The answer is simple: Jesus is talking within the framework of the common experience of his day, relating stories and examples based upon the people, business practices, and daily occurrences that those in his audience saw all around them, all the time.

If Jesus were here today, he would do the very same thing. He would speak about recovering alcoholics, stockbrokers, Sunday golfers, income tax returns, corporate shakeups, and a myriad of other things that are seen and experienced by you and me every day of our lives.

The format Jesus used to present more than one-third of his teaching, and with which this book is concerned, is known as a parable. And a parable, ranging from one sentence to a whole story, is simply a manner of teaching by way of comparison or analogy. The speaker endeavors to convey a single dramatic point to arouse the hearer into action, action that will result in furthering his own well-being and that of others as followers of God.

Over the years, daily common experience has changed radically; however, the moral principles and urgency of Christ's message have not changed or been affected by the passage of time, for Christ is the same yesterday, today, and tomorrow. Accordingly, the most productive manner in which to understand fully the dramatic point of each of Jesus' parables is to take Jesus' original point and set it within the framework of twentieth-century common experience. This is possible, and indeed a legitimate venture, because the holiness, efficacy, and validity of Scripture, especially as they relate to the parables, lie not so much in the stories themselves, as they do in the point that each of these stories is intending to convey.

And so, as you study each of these parables with a view to the original text of Scripture, hopefully they will prove to be for you a key to unlock the treasury of Christ's powerful and intensely practical pronouncements on life, death, and everyday living. But even more, with your new insight into the meaning of Christ's teaching, perhaps you will be inspired to write some parables of your own, which will apply the point of Jesus' parables to the daily life experiences you encounter. In so doing, the gospel of Jesus Christ will come alive in new and exciting ways.

Carl G. Carlozzi, D.Min.

*And Jesus looked around and said to his
disciples, "How hard it will be for those
who have riches to enter the kingdom of
God!" And the disciples were amazed at
his words.*

*But Jesus said to them again, "Chil-
dren, how hard it is to enter the kingdom
of God! It is easier for a camel to go
through the eye of a needle than for a rich
man to enter the kingdom of God."* (Mark
10:23-25)

And Jesus looked around and said to his
disciples, "How hard it will be for the af-
fluent of this world, with their wealth and
power, to enter the kingdom of God!"
And the disciples were amazed at his
words.

But Jesus said to them again, "Boys,
how hard it is to enter the kingdom of
God! It is easier for a semitrailer to drive
through the center of a Cheerio than for
a man with wealth and power to enter
the kingdom of God."

11

"Listen! A sower went out to sow. And as he sowed, some seed fell along the path, and the birds came and devoured it. Other seed fell on rocky ground, where it had not much soil, and immediately it sprang up, since it had no depth of soil; and when the sun rose it was scorched, and since it had no root it withered away. Other seed fell among thorns and the thorns grew up and choked it, and it yielded no grain. And other seeds fell into good soil and brought forth grain, growing up and increasing and yielding thirtyfold and sixtyfold and a hundredfold."

And he said, "He who has ears to hear, let him hear." (Mark 4:3-9)

"Listen! An investor went out to increase his net worth. And as he invested, he put some money into a new franchise, but poor management devoured his investment. Other funds he put into bonds, and as they began to

12

make him money, interest rates rose, and his investment withered away. Other money was invested in speculative stocks, but when a recession began, it retarded projected growth, and they yielded no gain. But other funds were invested in good real estate and in a diversified portfolio of blue chip stocks and brought forth gain, growing up and increasing 30 percent and 60 percent and 100 percent."

And he said, "He who has ears to hear, let him hear."

RECOVERING ALCOHOLIC

"When the unclean spirit has gone out of a man, he passes through waterless places seeking rest; and finding none he says, 'I will return to my house from which I came.' And when he comes he finds it swept and put in order. Then he goes and

brings seven other spirits more evil than himself, and they enter and dwell there; and the last state of that man becomes worse than the first." (Luke 11:24-26)

"When an alcoholic begins to recover, he makes it a point to stay out of bars as he seeks companionship; and often finding none among strangers, he says, 'I will go back to my neighborhood tavern, but only to talk with my friends.' But after he is there for a while, and he perceives he is handling the situation well, he begins to rationalize that he can have just one drink to be sociable. Then he goes and has another drink, and another, and another, and he becomes drunk again; and the last state of that man becomes worse than the first."

THE ECONOMIC TRENDS

"When you see a cloud rising in the west, you say at once, 'A shower is coming'; and so it happens. And when you see the

south wind blowing, you say, 'There will be scorching heat'; and it happens. You hypocrites! You know how to interpret the appearance of earth and sky; but why do you not know how to interpret the present time?" (Luke 12:54-56)

"When you see inflation on the rise, you say at once, 'The prime lending rate will go up'; and so it happens. And when you see the dollar is strong, you say, 'Foreign imports will increase'; and it happens. You hypocrites! You know how to interpret economic trends; but why do you not know how to interpret the present time?"

THE DRUG ADDICTS

"Can a blind man lead a blind man? Will they not both fall into a pit?" (Luke 6:39)

"Can a drug addict help his friend overcome his habit? Will they not both become junkies?"

15

"To what then shall I compare the men of this generation, and what are they like? They are like children sitting in the market place and calling to one another, 'We piped to you, and you did not dance; we wailed, and you did not weep.'" (Luke 7:31, 32)

"To what then shall I compare the men of this generation, and what are they like? They are like litigants in a lawsuit calling out to one another, 'We wanted to settle, and you wanted to go to court; so we determined to go to court, and you wanted to settle.'"

"The harvest is plentiful, but the laborers are few; pray therefore the Lord of the harvest to send out laborers into his harvest." (Luke 10:2)

"The unsaved are plentiful, but the evangelists are few; pray therefore the Lord of the unsaved to send out evangelists to the unsaved."

INCESSANT
PHONE CALLS

"Which of you who has a friend will go to him at midnight and say to him, 'Friend, lend me three loaves; for a friend of mine

17

has arrived on a journey, and I have nothing to set before him'; and he will answer from within, 'Do not bother me; the door is now shut, and my children are with me in bed; I cannot get up and give you anything'? I tell you, though he will not get up and give him anything because he is his friend, yet because of his importunity he will rise and give him whatever he needs." (Luke 11:5-8)

"Which of you, who has a husband, will telephone him at the office and wish to speak with him on a matter of domestic urgency; and his secretary will answer you, 'I'm sorry, but he is busy in a meeting and can't talk to you now'? I tell you, though he will not come out of the meeting because he is your husband, yet because of your repeated calls he will excuse himself from the meeting, pick up the phone, and give you whatever you desire."

"Two men went up into the temple to pray, one a Pharisee and the other a tax collector. The Pharisee stood and prayed thus with himself, 'God, I thank thee that I am not like other men, extortioners, unjust, adulterers, or even like this tax collector. I fast twice a week, I give tithes of all that I get.'

"But the tax collector, standing far off, would not even lift up his eyes to heaven, but beat his breast, saying, 'God, be merciful to me a sinner!'

"I tell you, this man went down to his house justified rather than the other; for every one who exalts himself will be humbled, but he who humbles himself will be exalted." (Luke 18:10-14)

"Two men went into a church during their lunch hour to pray, one a loyal church member and the other an acquaintance of his who played golf almost every Sunday morning. The church member knelt at the altar and prayed thus with himself, 'God, I thank you that I am not like other men, corrupt in business, neglectful in worship, adulterous in marriage, given to drinking to excess, or even like this Sunday golfer who rarely darkens your door, except for weddings, funerals, and Christmas and Easter. I go to Bible study twice a week, I make a generous pledge to support your church, and I sing in the choir.'

"But the Sunday golfer, kneeling in a pew toward the back of the church, would not even lift up his eyes to look at the cross, but anguishing in his mind, prayed, 'Lord, there is something missing in my life. I am just so miserable, and I need some help from you to turn my life around. I have sinned against you for too long.'

"I tell you, this man went back to his office in good standing before God rather than the other; for everyone who praises himself will be humbled, but he who humbles himself will be praised."

"As you go with your accuser before the magistrate, make an effort to settle with him on the way, lest he drag you to the judge, and the judge hand you over to the officer, and the officer put you in prison. I tell you, you will never get out till you have paid the very last copper." (Luke 12:58, 59)

"If you, as a defendant, are headed for trial and know you are going to lose, make an effort to settle out of court with the plaintiff, lest he win his suit, and the judge put a lien on your property, and your wages be garnisheed. I tell you, you will never get out of this mess until you have paid the very last dollar."

"There was a rich man who had a steward, and charges were brought to him that this man was wasting his goods. And he called him and said to him, 'What is this that I hear about you? Turn in the account of your stewardship, for you can no longer be steward.'

"And the steward said to himself, 'What shall I do, since my master is taking the stewardship away from me? I am not strong enough to dig, and I am ashamed to beg. I have decided what to do, so that people may receive me into their houses when I am put out of the stewardship.'

"So, summoning his master's debtors one by one, he said to the first, 'How much do you owe my master?'

"He said, 'A hundred measures of oil.'

"And he said to him, 'Take your bill, and sit down quickly and write fifty.'

Then he said to another, 'And how much do you owe?'

"He said, 'A hundred measures of wheat.'

"He said to him, 'Take your bill, and write eighty.'

"The master commended the dishonest steward for his prudence; for the sons of this world are wiser in their own generation than the sons of light." (Luke 16:1-8)

"There was a rich man who had an estate manager, and charges were brought to him that this man was skimming funds. And his employer called him and said, 'I am going to order an independent audit, and if what I hear is true, you are going to be fired!'

"And the estate manager said to himself, 'If I lose this job, my reputation will be ruined and no one will hire me; and I certainly don't relish looking for a new occupation. I know what I will do to keep my name in the clear.'

"So, sitting down in his office, he called in his employer's debtors, one by one, and said to them, 'I am in a bit of a jam from which we can both benefit if you will keep your mouth shut and cooperate. I have altered my books and reduced the amount due on your account by 20 percent, and I would like you to make the necessary adjustments in your books.'

"And the rich man commended the dishonest estate manager for his shrewdness and resourcefulness in the face of impending judgment; for worldly people are often more shrewd in their dealings than are most godly people."

THE MARKETING TECHNIQUE

"You are the light of the world. A city set on a hill cannot be hid." (Matthew 5:14)

"You are the neon of the world. A product advertised on a flashing billboard cannot go unnoticed."

"Who then is the faithful and wise steward, whom his master will set over his household, to give them their portion of food at the proper time? Blessed is that servant whom his master when he comes will find so doing. Truly I tell you, he will set him over all his possessions.

"But if that servant says to himself, 'My master is delayed in coming,' and begins to beat the menservants and the maidservants, and to eat and drink and get drunk, the master of that servant will come on a day when he does not expect him and at an hour he does not know, and will punish him, and put him with the unfaithful." (Luke 12:42-46)

"Who then is the faithful and wise account executive, whom his client will put in charge of his stock portfolio, to buy and sell at the proper time? Fortunate is that broker whom his client finds keeping abreast of market trends and making trades to his best advantage. Truly, I tell you, he will give his broker all of his investment business.

"But if that broker thinks to himself, 'That man does not fully comprehend the market, and he trusts what I tell him without doing any research himself,' and he begins to churn his account so he enjoys more commissions, the client of that broker will one day find out; and quite unexpectedly, he will withdraw his account and spread the word to others about this account executive's disreputable practices."

THE NEW HOUSE

"For which of you, desiring to build a tower, does not first sit down and count the cost, whether he has enough to complete it? Otherwise, when he has laid a foundation, and is not able to finish, all who see it begin to mock him, saying, 'This man began to build, and was not able to finish.'" (Luke 14:28-30)

"For which of you, desiring to build a new house, does not first get bids and determine, with the financing available to you, whether you can afford to complete the project. Otherwise, when the shell is erected and half of the finish work done, and you are not able to pay the subcontractors, your friends are heard to say at parties, 'That man was not very astute. He started to build a house and did not plan ahead for contingencies.'"

THE CORPORATE SHAKE-UP

"*A nobleman went into a far country to receive a kingdom and then return. Calling ten of his servants, he gave them ten pounds, and said to them, 'Trade with these till I come.'*

"*But his citizens hated him and sent an embassy after him, saying, 'We do not want this man to reign over us.'*

"*When he returned, having received the kingdom, he commanded these servants, to whom he had given the money, to be* called to him, that he might know what they had gained by trading.

"The first came before him, saying, 'Lord, your pound has made ten pounds more.'

"And he said to him, 'Well done, good servant! Because you have been faithful in a very little, you shall have authority over ten cities.'

"And the second came, saying, 'Lord, your pound has made five pounds.'

"And he said to him, 'And you are to be over five cities.'

"Then another came, saying, 'Lord, here is your pound, which I have kept laid away in a napkin; for I was afraid of you, because you are a severe man; you take up what you did not lay down, and reap what you did not sow.'

"He said to him, 'I will condemn you out of your own mouth, you wicked servant! You knew that I was a severe man, taking up what I did not lay down and reaping what I did not sow? Why then did you not put my money into the bank, and at my coming I should have collected it with interest?' And he said to those who stood by, 'Take the pound from him, and give it to him who has the ten pounds.'

"(And they said to him, 'Lord, he has ten pounds!')

"'I tell you that to every one who has will more be given; but from him who has not, even what he has will be taken away. But as for these enemies of mine, who did not want me to reign over them, bring them here and slay them before me.'"
(Luke 19:12-27)

"The chairman of a large corporation was planning an extended trip abroad to enter into very difficult negotiations for what could become a most profitable acquisition. And calling in his five subsidiary presidents, he said, 'For the period of time I will be out of the country, I give you full decision-making power over each of your subsidiaries. I expect full attention to detail, decisive management, visionary leadership, and no foul-ups!'

"Now, during his absence, three of his corporate directors, who disliked him because of his arrogant manner, said at a board meeting, 'This man is ruthless. He is simply an egocentric and vindictive tyrant who will ruin this company with his arbitrary decisions and pipe-dream ideas for new acquisitions. We think he should be replaced!'

"When the chairman returned from abroad, having negotiated the most successful acquisition in the company's history, he called a meeting of his subsidiary presidents, demanding full reports on the progress each had made during his absence.

"The first president to report to him said, 'Your paper products subsidiary has experienced a 10 percent increase in sales.'

"And the chairman replied, 'Just as I had expected. You have done well. I can see a bright future for you in my employ.'

"And the second president said, 'The foods subsidiary has shown a 5 percent increase in sales.'

"And to him the chairman replied, 'You have exercised good administrative ability. I can see that you will be with me for some time.'

"Then another reported to him, saying, 'The plastics subsidiary lost in the bidding on that new contract we wanted. Now this happened because I was reluctant to lower our bid price in that it might have had some adverse effects on our year-end corporate profits; and I did not want to take a chance on either that or on upsetting you.'

"To which the chairman replied, 'You idiot! Just what do you think I do every day in running this company? I take calculated risks. Likewise, you should have taken that risk of lowering the bid, for the potential temporary loss would have been far offset by future sales in the form of spin-off business.' And he said to those at the table, 'I am going to order a reorganization and place the plastics business under the control of the paper products subsidiary, for there we have got some management with vision and initiative.'

"(And those in the room said to him, 'That subsidiary already is doing $40 million a year in business!')

"And the chairman said, 'I tell you, that every one who has initiative, to him will more be given; but to him who shows no initiative, even what he has will be taken away.' Then the chairman said to those at the table, 'And now, as for those directors who impugned my administrative ability, at the next meeting of the board I am going to call for a vote to have them removed.'"

"And no one puts new wine into old wine-skins; if he does, the wine will burst the skins, and the wine is lost, and so are the skins; but new wine is for fresh skins." (Mark 2:22)

"And no one teaches new math concepts with old teaching tools; if he does, the new math confuses the students, the teaching is lost, and so are the students; for new concepts require a fresh approach."

THE COMMERCIAL JINGLE

"To what shall I compare the kingdom of God? It is like leaven which a woman took and hid in three measures of flour, till it was all leavened." (Luke 13:20, 21)

"To what shall I compare the kingdom of God? It is like a commercial jingle which a man hums in his office, till everyone else in the room is humming it."

THE FLAT BEVERAGE

"*Salt is good; but if the salt has lost its saltness, how will you season it? Have salt in yourselves, and be at peace with one another.*" (Mark 9:50)

"Carbonated soft drinks are good; but if the carbonation is lost, what good is the beverage? Have sparkle in your lives, and be at peace with one another."

LAW SCHOOL GRADUATE

"*When a woman is in travail she has sorrow, because her hour has come; but when she is delivered of the child, she no*

*longer remembers the anguish, for joy that
a child is born into the world."* (John
16:21)

"When a law school graduate is cram-
ming for the bar examination, she experiences tremendous tension and anxiety
because her future career is on the line;
but when she receives notice that she
has passed the bar, she no longer remembers the anguish, for joy that she
can now practice law."

THE PRIVATE SCHOOL

*"I am the true vine, and my Father is the
vinedresser. Every branch of mine that
bears no fruit, he takes away, and every
branch that does bear fruit he prunes, that
it may bear more fruit. You are already
made clean by the word which I have spoken to you. Abide in me, and I in you. As
the branch cannot bear fruit by itself, unless it abides in the vine, neither can you,
unless you abide in me.*

"I am the vine, you are the branches. He who abides in me, and I in him, he it is that bears much fruit, for apart from me you can do nothing. If a man does not abide in me, he is cast forth as a branch and withers; and the branches are gathered, thrown into the fire and burned. If you abide in me, and my words abide in you, ask whatever you will, and it shall be done for you.

"By this my Father is glorified, that you bear much fruit, and so prove to be my disciples. As the Father has loved me, so have I loved you; abide in my love. If you keep my commandments, you will abide in my love, just as I have kept my Father's commandments and abide in his love. These things I have spoken to you, that my joy may be in you, and that your joy may be full." (John 15:1-11)

"I am the best private school, and my Father is the headmaster. Every student of mine that does not maintain his grades and abide by the rules, he expels, and every student that does maintain his grades and abide by the rules he challenges, that he may excel to greater heights of excellence in academics and character. You have already been made one of my students by the word I have spoken to you. Take me seriously and I will take you seriously. As the student cannot attain to full excellence of academic achievement and character by himself, unless he stays in school, neither can you, unless you stay enrolled in my private school.

"I am the best private school, you are the students. He who stays in my school, and receives my instruction, he it is who will truly excel in life, for without this academic training and character building, you will not amount to very much. If a student does not work hard to remain in my school, he will be expelled by the headmaster as a failure and will lack confidence in himself; and the failures in life tend to associate with one another, and are eaten alive by a competitive and success-oriented world. So, if you stay in my school, and my teaching sinks into your head, ask whatever you will, and my Father, the headmaster, will go out of his way to help you.

"By this my Father is honored, that you succeed in life, and so prove to be my alumni. As the headmaster has loved me, so I have loved you; stay a faithful and active alumni. If you keep putting into practice what you have learned here, you will go on succeeding in life, just as I have kept my standards of excellence high and have my Father's approval. These things I have spoken to you, that my joy may be in seeing you grow up to become true successes in life, and that your joy may be in enjoying the fruits of that success for yourself."

THE AUTO MECHANIC

"Will any one of you, who has a servant plowing or keeping sheep, say to him when he has come in from the field, 'Come at once and sit down at table'?

"Will he not rather say to him, 'Prepare supper for me, and gird yourself and serve me, till I eat and drink; and afterward you shall eat and drink'?

"Does he thank the servant because he did what was commanded? So you also, when you have done all that is commanded you, say, 'We are unworthy servants; we have only done what was our duty.'" (Luke 17:7-10)

"Will the owner of any auto dealership, who has a mechanic in the midst of a busy day's work, say to him, 'Pull that customer's car out of the service bay and drive in your own car and fix what needs to be done on company time'?

"Will he not rather say to him, 'Do the work you have been hired to do for my customers; and after the garage closes, you may use my facilities to repair your own car'?

"Does the owner of that auto dealership go out and thank the employee each day for doing what he is expected to do? So also, when you have done all that is expected of you, say, 'We are unworthy followers; we have only done what was our duty.'"

THE TRUSTWORTHY FATHER

"What father among you, if his son asks for a fish, will instead of a fish give him a serpent; or if he asks for an egg, will give him a scorpion? If you then, who are evil, know how to give good gifts to your chil-

dren, how much more will the heavenly Father give the Holy Spirit to those who ask him!" (Luke 11:11-13)

"What father among you, if his daughter asks to use the car, will let her have it if he knows that the brakes are defective; or if she asks to borrow money to assist with her college expenses, will give her a worthless check? If you then, who are evil, know how to give good gifts to your children, how much more will your Father in heaven do for you who are also his child?"

THE TERRIBLE TENANTS

"A man planted a vineyard, and set a hedge around it, and dug a pit for the wine press, and built a tower, and let it out to tenants, and went into another country.

"When the time came, he sent a servant to the tenants, to get from them some of the fruit of the vineyard. And they took

*him and beat him, and sent him away
empty-handed.*

*"Again he sent to them another servant,
and they wounded him in the head, and
treated him shamefully. And he sent another, and him they killed; and so with
many others, some they beat and some
they killed.*

*"He had still one other, a beloved son;
finally he sent him to them, saying, 'They
will respect my son.'*

*"But those tenants said to one another,
'This is the heir; come, let us kill him,
and the inheritance will be ours.' And they
took him and killed him, and cast him out
of the vineyard.*

*"What will the owner of the vineyard
do? He will come and destroy the tenants,
and give the vineyard to others."* (Mark
12:1-10)

"A builder from another city came to a
new area, built an apartment complex,
put in a swimming pool, landscaped the
property nicely, let it out to tenants, and
returned to his hometown.

"When the rent came due and nothing
came to him, he sent notices by mail, but
most of the tenants ignored them. Next
he sent registered letters, but these
same tenants simply tore them up. Next

he sent one of his employees, and those tenants gave him a lot of excuses and verbal abuse.

"And finally, he sent his only son, saying, 'They will listen to him and show him some respect, and get in line by paying the rent.'

"But those tenants said to one another, 'This is the owner's son; if we can get rid of him by driving him off, we can live rent-free for a while longer.' And those tenants ganged up on him, beat him, and he died.

"What will the owner of that apartment complex do? He will come and have those tenants arrested and evicted, and rent the apartments to others."

THE CLOTHING STORE

"A man had a fig tree planted in his vineyard; and he came seeking fruit on it and found none. And he said to the vinedresser, 'Lo, these three years I have come seeking fruit on this fig tree, and I find none.

Cut it down; why should it use up the ground?'

"*And he answered him, 'Let it alone, sir, this year also, till I dig about it and put on manure. And if it bears fruit next year, well and good; but if not, you can cut it down.'*" (Luke 13:6-9)

"An investor purchased a clothing store in a shopping mall; and he came seeking profit and found none. And he said to his manager, 'For three years I have come looking for this store to show a profit, and yet it hasn't. I've decided to close it; why should I waste my money?'

"And the manager answered him, 'Let me have one more year, sir, as I have some new ideas concerning advertising and display. And if they work in this coming year, well and good; but if not, you can close the doors.'"

"But know this, that if the householder had known at what hour the thief was coming, he would not have left his house to be broken into." (Luke 12:39)

"But know this, if the bank manager had known at what time the robbery was going to take place, he would have arranged for a police stakeout and not allowed the robbery to occur."

"The eye is the lamp of the body. So, if your eye is sound, your whole body will be full of light; but if your eye is not sound, your whole body will be full of darkness. If

*then the light in you is darkness, how
great is the darkness!"* (Matthew 6:22,
23)

"Your integrity is the foundation of all
your relationships. So, if your integrity is
sound, all of your relationships will be full
of dynamic potential; but if your integrity
is questionable, all of your relationships
will be lacking. If then you lack integrity,
the magnitude of your personal loss is
immeasurable."

THE POLITICIAN

*"Therefore every scribe who has been
trained for the kingdom of heaven is like a
householder who brings out of his treasure
what is new and what is old."* (Matthew
13:52)

"Therefore every theologian who has
been trained for the kingdom of heaven
is like a politician who is able to meet

contemporary issues with an open mind, but is also ready to stand firm for the true values and principles of the past."

RING AROUND THE COLLAR

"For no good tree bears bad fruit, nor again does a bad tree bear good fruit; for each tree is known by its own fruit. For figs are not gathered from thorns, nor are grapes picked from a bramble bush.

"The good man out of the good treasure of his heart produces good, and the evil man out of his evil treasure produces evil; for out of the abundance of the heart his mouth speaks." (Luke 6:43-45)

"For no good laundry detergent leaves stains on a shirt collar, nor does an inferior detergent get these stains out; for each product is known by its effectiveness. For cleanliness is not obtained from dirt, nor is softness obtained from industrial cleansers.

"The good man out of a character based in ethical principles produces

45

good, and the evil man out of a character based in unethical principles produces evil; for a man's words and actions reveal his true character."

THE NUCLEAR ARMS RACE

"*And there will be signs in sun and moon and stars, and upon the earth distress of nations in perplexity at the roaring of the sea and the waves, men fainting with fear and with foreboding of what is coming on the world; for the powers of the heavens will be shaken. And then they will see the Son of man coming in a cloud with power and great glory. Now when these things begin to take place, look up and raise your heads, because your redemption is drawing near.*"

And he told them a parable: "Look at the fig tree, and all the trees; as soon as they come out in leaf, you see for yourselves and know that the summer is already near. So also, when you see these things taking place, you know that the kingdom of God is near." (Luke 21:25-31)

"And there will be signs in sun and moon and stars, and upon the earth nations will be in turmoil not unlike the raging of the sea in a severe storm, and many will lose both their self-confidence and their courage when they see what is happening in world affairs; for the powers of the heavens will be shaken. And then these same people will perceive that the second coming of Christ, with power and great glory, is no idle promise. Now when these things begin to take place, you, as believers, may face these events with confidence and hope, because your redemption is drawing near."

And Jesus told them a parable, saying, "Look at the nuclear arms buildup in your own nation, and in many other nations; and as one nation continues to challenge and threaten another, you see for yourselves and know the ever present danger of a nuclear holocaust. So, also, when you see these things beginning to happen, you know that the kingdom of God is near."

But he, desiring to justify himself, said to Jesus, "And who is my neighbor?"

Jesus replied, "A man was going down from Jerusalem to Jericho, and he fell among robbers, who stripped him and beat him, and departed, leaving him half dead.

"Now by chance a priest was going down that road; and when he saw him he passed by on the other side. So likewise a Levite, when he came to the place and saw him, passed by on the other side.

"But a Samaritan, as he journeyed, came to where he was; and when he saw him, he had compassion, and went to him and bound up his wounds, pouring on oil and wine; then he set him on his own beast and brought him to an inn, and took care of him. And the next day he took out two denarii and gave them to the innkeeper, saying, 'Take care of him; and whatever more you spend, I will repay you when I come back.'

"Which of these three, do you think,

proved neighbor to the man who fell among the robbers?"

He said, "The one who showed mercy on him."

And Jesus said to him, "Go and do likewise." (Luke 10:29-37)

But an attorney, desiring to justify himself, said to Jesus, "And who is my neighbor?"

Jesus replied, "A vagrant was hitchhiking from New York to Boston, and he was accosted by a group of teenagers, who robbed and beat him, and departed, leaving him bruised and bleeding.

"Now by chance a clergyman was driving down that road; and when he saw him he just kept on driving. So likewise, a born-again layman, when he came upon the scene, saw the vagrant lying on the side of the road, and he continued to drive on.

"But an atheist, as he drove along and came upon the man, had compassion, stopped his car, and administered what first aid he could. Then he put the vagrant into his car and drove to an emergency room at a nearby hospital. And he said to the nurse on duty, 'I doubt this man has any medical insurance, so let me pay you the emergency room charge now, and tomorrow I will come back and see what more I can do to assist him.' "

To the attorney, Jesus said, "Which of these three, do you think, proved a neighbor to the vagrant?"

He said, "The one who had compassion."

And Jesus replied, "Go and do likewise."

THE MASTERPIECE PAINTING

"Again, the kingdom of heaven is like a merchant in search of fine pearls, who, on finding one pearl of great value, went and sold all that he had and bought it." (Matthew 13:45, 46)

"Again, the kingdom of heaven is like an art collector in search of fine paintings, who, on finding a Rembrandt, went and sold all of his collection and bought it."

"No one sews a piece of unshrunk cloth on an old garment; if he does, the patch tears away from it, the new from the old, and a worse tear is made." (Mark 2:21)

"No president of a country combines his new program of foreign policy with the outdated policy of his predecessor; if he does, his accommodation will so distort it, the new from the old, that a worse breach of foreign relations will be made."

THE STING OPERATION

"But no one can enter a strong man's house and plunder his goods, unless he first binds the strong man; then indeed he may plunder his house." (Mark 3:27)

"But the F.B.I. cannot carry out a sting operation and get an indictment, unless it first infiltrates the organization of the criminal; then indeed it may bring him to trial."

THE CORPORATE LAWSUIT

"Or what king, going to encounter another king in war, will not sit down first and take counsel whether he is able with

*ten thousand to meet him who comes
against him with twenty thousand? And if
not, while the other is yet a great way off,
he sends an embassy and asks terms of
peace."* (Luke 14:31, 32)

"Or what corporation, as the defendant
in a lawsuit, will not first have its attor-
neys sit down and take counsel whether
they, with a weak case, are going to be
enabled to prevail over the plaintiff who
has a stronger case? And if not, before
the case comes to trial, the general
counsel of that firm goes and seeks an
out-of-court settlement."

THE BASEBALL FANS

*"Can the wedding guests fast while the
bridegroom is with them? As long as they
have the bridegroom with them, they cannot fast. The days will come, when the*

bridegroom is taken away from them, and then they will fast in that day." (Mark 2:19, 20)

"Can baseball fans be quiet when their team hits a home run? As long as their team is winning, they cannot be gloomy. The day will come, however, when their team will lose and enter a slump, and then they will be sad in that day."

THE HEADLIGHTS

"Nor do men light a lamp and put it under a bushel, but on a stand, and it gives light to all in the house." (Matthew 5:15)

"Nor do men turn on the headlights in their cars and then cover them up; but rather, they leave their headlights unobstructed so they, and others, can see where they are going."

"Therefore the kingdom of heaven may be compared to a king who wished to settle accounts with his servants.

"When he began the reckoning, one was brought to him who owed him ten thousand talents; and as he could not pay, his lord ordered him to be sold, with his wife and children and all that he had, and payment to be made.

"So the servant fell on his knees, imploring him, 'Lord, have patience with me, and I will pay you everything.' And out of pity for him the lord of that servant released him and forgave him the debt.

"But that same servant, as he went out, came upon one of his fellow servants who owed him a hundred denarii; and seizing him by the throat he said, 'Pay what you owe.'

"So his fellow servant fell down and besought him, 'Have patience with me, and I will pay you.' He refused and went and

*put him in prison till he should pay the
debt.*

*"When his fellow servants saw what
had taken place, they were greatly dis-
tressed, and they went and reported to
their lord all that had taken place. Then
his lord summoned him and said to him,
'You wicked servant! I forgave you all that
debt because you besought me; and should
not you have had mercy on your fellow
servant, as I had mercy on you?' And in
anger his lord delivered him to the jailers,
till he should pay all his debt.*

*"So also my heavenly Father will do to
every one of you, if you do not forgive your
brother from your heart."* (Matthew
18:23-35)

"Therefore the kingdom of heaven may
be compared to the owner of a lumberyard who wished to settle accounts with
his customers.

"And when he had begun, a building
contractor came to him who owed him
ten thousand dollars; but as he was not
able to pay, the lumberyard owner obtained a judgment and put a lien on his
house, demanding that payment be made
or his house would be sold to pay the
judgment.

"Now the contractor returned to the

owner's office, saying, 'Please have patience with me! The economy is in a shambles, and I have very little work. Allow me to pay you only the interest for the time being, and when the economy improves, I will pay you the principal in its entirety.' Then the owner of the lumberyard was moved with compassion, agreed to the contractor's proposal, and had the judgment against him lifted.

"But that same building contractor went out and found one of his own customers who owed him twenty-five hundred dollars; and he confronted him saying, 'I need the money you owe me, and I want it now!'

"So the homeowner, a real estate broker who was experiencing hard times, pleaded with him, saying, 'Have patience with me, and as soon as the economy improves I will pay you in full.' But the contractor would hear none of this, took him to court, obtained a judgment, and put a lien on his house.

"Now word of this came to the attention of the lumberyard owner, and he was furious. So the next day he went to the contractor's office and said to him, 'What kind of a miserable scoundrel are you? I delayed your payment to me because of your plight; should not you have done the same for one of your customers? OK, fair is fair! You will be hearing from my attorney in the morning; so, count on going back into court and losing your shirt, and that is putting it mildly!'

"So also my heavenly Father will do to every one of you, if you do not deal compassionately with your fellowman from your heart."

THE PERFECT FOOD

"I am the bread of life. Your fathers ate the manna in the wilderness, and they died. This is the bread which comes down from heaven, that a man may eat of it and not die. I am the living bread which came down from heaven; if any one eats of this bread, he will live for ever; and the bread which I shall give for the life of the world is my flesh." (John 6:48-51)

"I am the perfect food of life. Your ancestors ate ordinary food in the course of their lives, and they died. This is the perfect food which comes down from heaven, that a man may eat of it and be enabled to go on living even after his earthly body stops functioning. I am the perfect food which came down from heaven; if anyone eats this food, he will live forever; and the perfect food which I shall give for the life of the world is my flesh."

THE TWO EMPLOYEES

"A certain creditor had two debtors; one owed five hundred denarii, and the other fifty. When they could not pay, he forgave them both. Now which of them will love him more?"

Simon answered, "The one, I suppose,

to whom he forgave more."

And he said to him, "You have judged rightly." (Luke 7:41-43)

"A certain store owner had two employees; one was caught altering the books to hide the hundred dollars he had taken, and the other taking change out of the cash register to buy a cup of coffee. When they had apologized for their indiscretions, he forgave them both. Now which of them will love him more?"

Simon answered, "The one, I suppose, to whom he forgave more."

And Jesus said to him, "You have answered correctly."

THE HARDWARE STORE

"For the kingdom of heaven is like a householder who went out early in the morning to hire laborers for his vineyard. After agreeing with the laborers for a den-

*arius a day, he sent them into his vine-
yard.*

"And going out about the third hour he
saw others standing idle in the market
place; and to them he said, 'You go into
the vineyard too, and whatever is right I
will give you.' So they went.

"Going out again about the sixth hour
and the ninth hour, he did the same. And
about the eleventh hour he went out and
found others standing; and he said to
them, 'Why do you stand here idle all
day?'

"They said to him, 'Because no one has
hired us.'

"He said to them, 'You go into the vineyard too.'

"And when evening came, the owner of
the vineyard said to his steward, 'Call the
laborers and pay them their wages, beginning with the last, up to the first.' And
when those hired about the eleventh hour
came, each of them received a denarius.

"Now when the first came, they thought
they would receive more; but each of them
also received a denarius. And on receiving
it they grumbled at the householder, saying, 'These last worked only one hour,
and you have made them equal to us who
have borne the burden of the day and
scorching heat.'

"But he replied to one of them, 'Friend, I am doing you no wrong; did you not agree with me for a denarius? Take what belongs to you, and go; I choose to give to this last as I give to you. Am I not allowed to do what I choose with what belongs to me? Or do you begrudge my generosity?'

"So the last will be first, and the first last." (Matthew 20:1-16)

"For the kingdom of heaven is like a small town merchant who, in opening a hardware store, began to search for reliable employees to staff his store. And after finding his first two employees, and agreeing with them on wages and benefits, he welcomed them into the business.

"Now, after three years of operation he found it necessary to hire an additional employee; and he said to him, after agreeing with him on wages and benefits, 'I am glad to have you as a part of my business.'

"As the business continued to prosper, the owner found it necessary to add an additional employee in the sixth, ninth, and eleventh years of the store's operation; and with each new employee, after agreeing on wages and benefits, he said, 'I am truly delighted to have you as a part of my family of employees.'

"Two years thereafter the merchant reached the age of retirement and sold the store. And calling his employees together, beginning with the most recently hired and continuing on to the longest employed, he said, 'You have been most loyal. Thanks to your diligent efforts over the years, you have enabled me to make my business a resounding success.' As a way of expressing his gratitude, he said to each one, 'I have sold my business for a great deal of money and I would like you to share in my good fortune by accepting this check for three thousand dollars.'

"Now the next day the merchant heard rumors of grumbling and resentment on the part of the employees hired at the beginning. And calling them into his office, he said, 'Why are you so displeased with what I have done?'

"They said to him, 'We do not think you have been fair! While some of these people have only worked here four or five years, we have been with you since the beginning. We think we should have received more than they did in recognition of our long years of service.'

"But he said to them, 'Just wait a minute! I never cheated you on your wages

63

and benefits, and I certainly never committed myself to any bonus or profit-sharing plan if I sold the store. Take your checks and go; I have chosen to reward all of you equally. Am I somehow prohibited from doing what I choose with the good fortune that is mine? Or do you begrudge my generosity?'

"So the last will be first, and the first last."

BELIEVERS AND UNBELIEVERS

"Those who are well have no need of a physician, but those who are sick; I came not to call the righteous, but sinners." (Mark 2:17)

"Those who believe have no need to be evangelized, but those who do not believe; I came not to call believers, but unbelievers."

*"The kingdom of heaven is like a net
which was thrown into the sea and gathered fish of every kind; when it was full,
men drew it ashore and sat down and
sorted the good into vessels but threw away
the bad.*

*"So it will be at the close of the age. The
angels will come out and separate the evil
from the righteous, and throw them into
the furnace of fire; there men will weep
and gnash their teeth."* (Matthew
13:47-50)

"The kingdom of heaven is like the Inter-
nal Revenue Service which sent out
forms across the country and gathered in
returns from every kind of person.

"When April fifteenth had passed, the
examiners put the returns into the com-
puters, and then sat down and began to
look over the results; and those who had
filed an honest return were passed over,
but those who appeared to have de-

frauded the government were called in for an audit, and in many instances, retribution was had.

"So it will be at the close of the age. Christ will come again and separate those with integrity from those who have been deceitful. And the deceitful will be sent by him to hell; and there they will lament their stupidity and experience total anxiety and frustration."

QUESTIONABLE NEW MEMBERS

"The kingdom of heaven may be compared to a man who sowed good seed in his field; but while men were sleeping, his enemy came and sowed weeds among the wheat, and went away. So when the plants came up and bore grain, then the weeds appeared also. And the servants of the householder came and said to him, 'Sir, did you not sow good seed in your field? How then has it weeds?'

"He said to them, 'An enemy has done this.'

"The servants said to him, 'Then do you want us to go and gather them?'

"But he said, 'No; lest in gathering the weeds you root up the wheat along with them. Let both grow together until the harvest; and at harvest time I will tell the reapers, Gather the weeds first and bind them in bundles to be burned, but gather the wheat into my barn.'" (Matthew 13:24-30)

"The kingdom of heaven may be compared to a faithful parishioner who labored diligently to recruit upstanding new people for her church; but as the months went by, other parishioners brought in new members of rather diverse backgrounds. Some were businessmen of questionable reputation, others were alcoholics, two were thought to be homosexuals, several were known to have engaged in extramarital affairs, and many others showed no outward appearance of knowing the Lord.

"Upon discovering this, the faithful parishioner came to her clergyman and said, 'Pastor, just what kind of a church are we running? Why, I perceive there are notorious sinners in our midst! I even had to kneel at the communion rail this morning next to an adulterer. Just how did all of these people get in here?'

"And her pastor said to her, 'Your fellow parishioners have done this.'

"And she said to him, 'Would you like me to go and form a committee to investigate the matter and advise the board as to just who these sinners are?'

"But her pastor said, 'No; lest while you try to distinguish between the real saints and the real sinners you throw out some of God's own. Do this: Let both worship together until we are all called before God in eternity; and at the time of the judgment, God, I am sure, will single out the righteous from the unrighteous.'"

FOUR COLLEGE GIRLS

"Then the kingdom of heaven shall be compared to ten maidens who took their lamps and went to meet the bridegroom. Five of them were foolish, and five were

wise. For when the foolish took their lamps, they took no oil with them; but the wise took flasks of oil with their lamps.

"As the bridegroom was delayed, they all slumbered and slept. But at midnight there was a cry, 'Behold, the bridegroom! Come out to meet him.' Then all those maidens rose and trimmed their lamps.

"And the foolish said to the wise, 'Give us some of your oil, for our lamps are going out.'

"But the wise replied, 'Perhaps there will not be enough for us and for you; go rather to the dealers and buy for yourselves.'

"And while they went to buy, the bridegroom came, and those who were ready went in with him to the marriage feast; and the door was shut.

"Afterward the other maidens came also, saying, 'Lord, lord, open to us.'

"But he replied, 'Truly, I say to you, I do not know you.'

"Watch therefore, for you know neither the day nor the hour." (Matthew 25:1-13)

"The kingdom of heaven shall be compared to four college girls who drove into the city to attend a concert. Two of them were scatterbrained, and two of them were prudent. For when the scatterbrained left for the city, they took with them only enough money for their tickets and some refreshments; but the prudent brought sufficient funds to cover the unexpected.

"As the concert was postponed until the next evening, they went out partying and spent the night and the next day camping out with others in front of the auditorium. In the afternoon there came the announcement, 'Tickets are now on sale, cash only.'

"And the scatterbrained said to the prudent, 'We spent all our money last night partying. How about a loan?'

"But the prudent replied, 'We do not have enough left to buy our tickets and yours; you will have to go to a bank and cash a check.'

"And while they were gone cashing their checks, all the tickets were sold.

"Returning to the auditorium and finding the box office closed, they began pounding on the door and shouting, 'Let us in! Our friends are inside.'

"Upon hearing this, an officer standing nearby said to them, 'I am really sorry, girls, but all the tickets are gone, and there is no way anyone can help you.'

"Be alert therefore, for you know neither the day nor the hour."

"Why do you see the speck that is in your brother's eye, but do not notice the log that is in your own eye?

"Or how can you say to your brother, 'Brother, let me take out the speck that is in your eye,' when you yourself do not see the log that is in your own eye?

"You hypocrite, first take the log out of your own eye, and then you will see clearly to take out the speck that is in your brother's eye." (Luke 6:41, 42)

"Why are you quick to notice that your neighbor occasionally tells lies, but do not notice that you are being unfaithful in your marriage?

"Or how can you say to your neighbor, 'Friend, let me help you with this lying,' when you do not see your own adultery?

"You hypocrite, first straighten out your own life, and then you will be justified in giving ethical advice to others."

"A man once gave a great banquet, and invited many; and at the time for the banquet he sent his servant to say to those who had been invited, 'Come; for all is now ready.'

"But they all alike began to make excuses. The first said to him, 'I have bought a field, and I must go out and see it; I pray you, have me excused.'

"And another said, 'I have bought five yoke of oxen, and I go to examine them; I pray you, have me excused.'

"And another said, 'I have married a wife, and therefore I cannot come.' So the servant came and reported this to his master.

"Then the householder in anger said to his servant, 'Go out quickly to the streets and lanes of the city, and bring in the poor and maimed and blind and lame.'

"And the servant said, 'Sir, what you commanded has been done, and still there is room.'

"And the master said to the servant, 'Go out to the highways and hedges, and compel people to come in, that my house may be filled. For I tell you, none of those men who were invited shall taste my banquet.'" (Luke 14:16-24)

"A businessman decided to give a dinner party, and invited three of his associates and their wives. Now two days before the party, when no one had responded to the invitations, he said to his wife, 'Why don't you give those folks a call and see what is going on?'

"But when his wife reached them on the phone, they all began to make excuses. The first said, 'We are picking up our new car that day, and we want to go and try it out; please give us a raincheck.'

"And another said, 'We have just purchased a new home, and we need to go shopping for furnishings; please excuse us.'

"And another said, 'Our daughter is getting married in three weeks, and you know what a hassle that is; perhaps we could come another time.' So the wife told this to her husband.

"Then the husband, in total exasperation, said to her, 'We have made all these preparations for a fantastic dinner, why don't we do something radically different? You know those two old ladies that you visit at the nursing home, why don't you invite them?'

"And his wife replied, 'We will still have room for several more people.'

"And he said, 'Well, then, why not call the halfway house for ex-convicts where I am on the board and see if some of those men can come. I tell you this, those who were invited are never going to know just what they missed.'"

MISPLACED WEDDING RING

"Or what woman, having ten silver coins, if she loses one coin, does not light a lamp and sweep the house and seek diligently until she finds it? And when she has found it, she calls together her friends and neighbors, saying, 'Rejoice with me, for I

have found the coin which I had lost.'

"Just so, I tell you, there is joy before the angels of God over one sinner who repents." (Luke 15:8-10)

"Or what housewife, having a great deal of jewelry, if she loses her wedding ring, does not literally move every piece of furniture and search through every drawer and nook and cranny until she finds it. And when she has found it, she calls her husband and her best friend and exclaims with joy, 'You'll never believe it, but I found my ring. What a relief!'

"Just so, I tell you, there is great joy in heaven over one unbeliever who gives his life to Christ."

THE EVIL INFLUENCES

"Hear me, all of you, and understand: there is nothing outside a man which by going into him can defile him; but the things which come out of a man are what defile him."

And when he had entered the house, and left the people, his disciples asked him about the parable. And he said to them, "Then are you also without understanding? Do you not see that whatever goes into a man from outside cannot defile him, since it enters, not his heart but his stomach, and so passes on?" (Thus he declared all foods clean.)

And he said, "What comes out of a man is what defiles a man. For from within, out of the heart of man, come evil thoughts, fornication, theft, murder, adultery, coveting, wickedness, deceit, licentiousness, envy, slander, pride, foolishness. All these evil things come from within, and they defile a man." (Mark 7:14-23)

"Hear me, all of you, and understand: there is nothing outside a man which by going into him can defile him—not the reading of non-Christian literature, not alcohol, not the hearing of jokes, not dancing, not movies, not card playing; but the things which come out of a man are what defile him."

And when he had entered the house, and left the people, his disciples asked him about the parable. And he said to them, "Do you not understand this

76

either? Do you not see that simply partaking or not partaking of these kinds of activities, in and of themselves, is not what corrupts a person? For they are merely activities and not inherently good or evil." (Thus he declared all activities harmless.)

And he said, "A man's heartfelt motivations are what defile him. For from within, out of a heart yielded to temptation, come evil thoughts, fornication, theft, murder, adultery, coveting, wickedness, deceit, licentiousness, envy, slander, pride, foolishness. All these come from within, and they defile a person."

THE SUPREME COURT

"When the Son of man comes in his glory, and all the angels with him, then he will sit on his glorious throne. Before him will be gathered all the nations, and he will separate them one from another as a shepherd separates the sheep from the goats, and he will place the sheep at his right

hand, but the goats at the left.

"Then the King will say to those at his right hand, 'Come, O blessed of my Father, inherit the kingdom prepared for you from the foundation of the world; for I was hungry and you gave me food, I was thirsty and you gave me drink, I was a stranger and you welcomed me, I was naked and you clothed me, I was sick and you visited me, I was in prison and you came to me.'

"Then the righteous will answer him, 'Lord, when did we see thee hungry and feed thee, or thirsty and give thee drink? And when did we see thee a stranger and welcome thee, or naked and clothe thee? And when did we see thee sick or in prison and visit thee?'

"And the king will answer them, 'Truly, I say to you, as you did it to one of the least of these my brethren, you did it to me.'

"Then he will say to those at his left hand, 'Depart from me, you cursed, into the eternal fire prepared for the devil and his angels; for I was hungry and you gave me no food, I was thirsty and you gave me no drink, I was a stranger and you did not welcome me, naked and you did not clothe me, sick and in prison and you did not visit me.'

"Then they also will answer, 'Lord, when did we see thee hungry or thirsty or a stranger or naked or sick or in prison, and did not minister to thee?'

"Then he will answer them, 'Truly, I say to you, as you did it not to one of the least of these, you did it not to me.'

"And they will go away into eternal punishment, but the righteous into eternal life." (Matthew 25:31-46)

"When the Son of man comes, he will set up his own Supreme Court. Before him will be tried all people, and he will separate them one from another as a judge separates the innocent from the convicted.

"Then the Judge will say to the innocent, 'Go now and experience freedom, joy, and meaning for your lives in that state of existence prepared for you from the foundation of the world; for I was hungry and you gave me food, I was thirsty and you gave me drink, I was a stranger and you welcomed me, I was in rags and you clothed me, I was sick and you visited me, I was in prison and you came to see me.'

"Then the innocent will answer him, 'Lord, when did we see you hungry and feed you, or thirsty and give drink? And when did we see you a stranger and welcome you, or in rags and clothe you? And when did we see you sick or in prison and visit you?'

"And the Judge will say to them, 'Truly, I say to you, as you showed compassionate love and assisted anyone who was downtrodden, disgraced, or in need of help, you exercised compassionate love and assistance to me, and showed me respect.'

"Then he will say to the convicted, 'Go now and experience anxiety, frustration, and meaninglessness in that state of existence prepared for you from the foundation of the world; for I was hungry and you gave me no food, I was thirsty and you gave me no drink, I was a stranger and you did not welcome me, in rags and you did not clothe me, sick and in prison and you did not visit me.'

"Then they also will answer, 'Lord, when did we see you hungry or thirsty or a stranger or in rags or sick or in prison, and did not come to your aid?'

"Then he will answer them, 'Truly, I say to you, as you did not show compassionate love and give assistance to anyone who was downtrodden, disgraced, or in need of help, you did not exercise compassionate love and assistance to me, or show me respect.'

"And the convicted will go away into eternal punishment, but the innocent into eternal life."

THE FACTORY WORKERS

"Let your loins be girded and your lamps burning, and be like men who are waiting for their master to come home from the marriage feast, so that they may open to him at once when he comes and knocks. Blessed are those servants whom the master finds awake when he comes; truly, I say to you, he will gird himself and have them sit at table, and he will come and serve them. If he comes in the second watch, or in the third, and finds them so, blessed are those servants!" (Luke 12:35-38)

"Let your work be steady and your witnessing constant, and be like factory workers who realize that their employer is one who conducts unannounced spot checks on worker efficiency and productivity, so that when he walks into the plant they may greet him without embarrassment. Fortunate are those employees whom their employer finds working diligently when he comes; truly, I say to you, he will sit down at the bargaining table with a positive view of their worth and be all the more inclined to meet their contract requests. If he comes to check on the second shift, or the third shift, and finds these employees conscientiously at work, fortunate are they as well."

THE UNITED WAY

"What is the kingdom of God like? And to what shall I compare it? It is like a grain of mustard seed which a man took and sowed in his garden; and it grew and became a tree, and the birds of the air made nests in its branches." (Luke 13:18, 19)

"What is the kingdom of God like? And to what shall I compare it? It is like an idea which a man had for establishing a

United Way agency in his community; and he talked to other leaders in his city, and the idea became a reality, and that reality produced millions of dollars, and the needy of that city found assistance through the many social service organizations supported by that agency."

THE NAIVE ENTREPRENEUR

"Take heed, and beware of all covetousness; for a man's life does not consist in the abundance of his possessions."

And he told them a parable, saying, "The land of a rich man brought forth plentifully; and he thought to himself, 'What shall I do, for I have nowhere to store my crops?' And he said, 'I will do this: I will pull down my barns, and build larger ones; and there I will store all my grain and my goods. And I will say to my soul, Soul, you have ample goods laid up for many years; take your ease, eat, drink, be merry.'

"But God said to him, 'Fool! This night your soul is required of you; and the *things you have prepared, whose will they be?'*

"So is he who lays up treasure for himself, and is not rich toward God." (Luke 12:15-21)

"Pay attention, and make certain that your priorities are in proper order; for a man's life does not consist in the abundance of his possessions."

And he told them a parable, saying, "The business of a successful manufacturer experienced tremendous growth; and he thought to himself, 'What shall I do, for I have no room in my present facility to store or produce sufficient inventory to meet market demands?' And he said, 'I will do this: I will tear down my old plant and build a new one; and there I will be enabled to accommodate increased production, be more cost effective in my operation, and in so doing, corner the market and make millions. And when that takes place, I will really have it made for years to come; I will build a new home, vacation in Europe, and get that Ferrari I have always wanted.'

"But God said to him, 'Fool! This very night you are going to have a coronary and die; and all the things you have amassed, what good will they do you?'

"So is he who lays up treasure for himself, and is not rich toward God."

THE TWO SECRETARIES

"What do you think? A man had two sons; and he went to the first and said, 'Son, go and work in the vineyard today.'

"And he answered, 'I will not'; but afterward he repented and went.

"And he went to the second and said the same; and he answered, 'I go, sir,' but did not go.

"Which of the two did the will of his father?"

They said, "The first."

Jesus said to them, "Truly, I say to you, the tax collectors and the harlots go into the kingdom of God before you. For John came to you in the way of righteousness, and you did not believe him, but the tax collectors and the harlots believed him;

and even when you saw it, you did not afterward repent and believe him. " (Matthew 21:28-32)

"What do you think? An attorney had two secretaries; and he went to the first and said, 'I have a tremendous backlog of cases and I need you to work late a couple of nights this week to get the files in order.'

"And she answered, 'You have got to be kidding. I have plans and I am not going to change them'; but afterward, she thought things over and worked those nights.

"And he went to the second and said the same; and she answered, ' I would be glad to help out,' but she never showed up.

"Which of the two did the will of her employer?"

And those who heard this replied, "The first."

Jesus said to them, "Truly, I say to you who consider yourselves religious, the adulterers, corrupt businessmen, and all manner of evil doers will go into the kingdom of God before you. For your pastor kept telling you how important it was to give your life to Christ, and you did not take him seriously, but the adulterers, corrupt businessmen, prostitutes, and all manner of evil doers took him seriously; and even when you saw this happening in your church, you did not reconsider your attitude toward God and change your ways."

REAL ESTATE
DEVELOPERS

"Every one who comes to me and hears my words and does them, I will show you what he is like: he is like a man building a house, who dug deep, and laid the foundation upon rock; and when a flood arose, the stream broke against that house, and could not shake it, because it had been well built.

"But he who hears and does not do them is like a man who built a house on the ground without a foundation; against which the stream broke, and immediately it fell, and the ruin of that house was great." (Luke 6:47-49)

"Every one who comes to me and hears my words and does them, I will show you what he is like: he is like a developer, who in purchasing real estate, undergirded his project with sufficient investors, and thereby secured the project with adequate capital; and when a recession came, operating costs greatly exceeded projected cash flow, but because he had strong capital reserves, he weathered adverse market conditions.

"But he who hears my words and does not do them is like a developer who purchased real estate without adequate financial backing; against which the recession came, and immediately operating costs devoured his cash flow and depleted his financial reserves, and so his creditors were at his door and his business failed, and the ramifications of his bankruptcy were widespread."

"The kingdom of God is as if a man should scatter seed upon the ground, and should sleep and rise night and day, and the seed should sprout and grow, he knows not how. The earth produces of itself, first the blade, then the ear, then the full grain in the ear. But when the grain is ripe, at once he puts in the sickle, because the harvest has come." (Mark 4:26-29)

"The kingdom of God is as if a worker should contribute from his earnings to an IRA, and should labor year after year, and his account should grow, but he does not understand fully how this works. The initial investment produces of itself, first the interest, then more principal is added, then interest compounded upon accumulated principal and interest, and so it builds with each contribution. But when he reaches age sixty-five, at once he begins to put in his just claim, because his retirement has come."

THE TESTIMONIAL DINNER

"When you are invited by any one to a marriage feast, do not sit down in a place of honor, lest a more eminent man than you be invited by him and he who invited you both will come and say to you, 'Give place to this man,' and then you will begin with shame to take the lowest place.

"But when you are invited, go and sit in the lowest place, so that when your host comes he may say to you, 'Friend, go up higher'; then you will be honored in the presence of all who sit at table with you.

"For every one who exalts himself will be humbled, and he who humbles himself will be exalted." (Luke 14:8-11)

"When someone invites you to a testimonial dinner, sit where you find your name card. Do not move the name cards around, for a more distinguished guest than yourself may perceive that he has been displaced; and the arrangements chairman will come and say to you, 'I think you are in the wrong seat,' and with great embarrassment you will be shown to another table further back in the hall.

"But when you are invited to a testimonial dinner, go and sit where you were intended to be seated, so that when your friend, the guest of honor, desires to give you recognition, he may call out, 'And now, I would like a man who has been a trusted friend over the years to come up and be at my side!' Then, as you come forward through the crowd, you will have the greater honor of all at the banquet.

"For he who tries to advance himself will be put down, but he who humbles himself will be honored."

And he told them a parable, to the effect that they ought always to pray and not lose heart.

He said, "In a certain city there was a judge who neither feared God nor regarded man; and there was a widow in that city who kept coming to him and saying, 'Vindicate me against my adversary.'

"For a while he refused; but afterward he said to himself, 'Though I neither fear God nor regard man, yet because this widow bothers me, I will vindicate her, or she will wear me out by her continual coming.'"

And the Lord said, "Hear what the unrighteous judge says. And will not God vindicate his elect, who cry to him day and night? Will he delay long over them? I tell you, he will vindicate them speedily. Nevertheless, when the Son of man comes, will he find faith on earth?" (Luke 18:1-8)

And he told them a parable, to the effect that they should always keep praying and never lose heart.

He said, "In a certain city there was a landlord who neither believed in God nor had any compassion for his tenants; and there was a widow, one of his tenants, who kept calling and sending him letters, saying, 'Do something about these awful conditions! The plumbing in this apartment is leaking and the furnace needs to be repaired.'

"For a while he refused; but after a time he said to himself, 'Though I couldn't care less about being known as a good Christian in the community, or worrying about the needs of that cranky old lady, yet because she is such a bother, I will fix up her apartment and tend to her needs or she may incite a tenants' strike among her neighbors.'"

And the Lord said, "Hear what the insensitive landlord says. And will not God also vindicate his followers, who cry to him day and night? Will he long postpone helping them? I tell you, he will come rapidly to their aid. Nevertheless, when Christ comes again, will he find faith on earth?"

"There was a rich man, who was clothed in purple and fine linen and who feasted sumptuously every day. And at his gate lay a poor man named Lazarus, full of sores, who desired to be fed with what fell from the rich man's table; moreover the dogs came and licked his sores.

"The poor man died and was carried by the angels to Abraham's bosom. The rich man also died and was buried; and in Hades, being in torment, he lifted up his eyes, and saw Abraham far off and Lazarus in his bosom. And he called out, 'Father Abraham, have mercy upon me, and send Lazarus to dip the end of his finger in water and cool my tongue; for I am in anguish in this flame.'

"But Abraham said, 'Son, remember that you in your lifetime received your good things, and Lazarus in like manner evil things; but now he is comforted here, and you are in anguish. And besides all this, between us and you a great chasm

has been fixed, in order that those who would pass from here to you may not be able, and none may cross from there to us.'

"And he said, 'Then I beg you, father, to send him to my father's house, for I have five brothers, so that he may warn them, lest they also come into this place of torment.'

"But Abraham said, 'They have Moses and the prophets; let them hear them.'

"And he said, 'No, father Abraham; but if some one goes to them from the dead, they will repent.'

"He said to him, 'If they do not hear Moses and the prophets, neither will they be convinced if some one should rise from the dead.'" (Luke 16:19-31)

"There was a physician's wife, who was clothed in designer jeans and polo shirts and who frequently dined in fine restaurants with her husband. And in her employ was a cleaning lady named Barbara, a recipient of food stamps and aid to dependent children, who was desperately seeking to earn a living for her family; moreover, the bill collectors were at her door and her children were constantly in need of the basic necessities of life.

"Now as the years passed by both

grew old and eventually departed this life. The cleaning lady found herself in eternity with Abraham and the faithful who had been resurrected. The physician's wife found herself separated from God and in misery in a place where God was not present. And being in anguish and experiencing an existence without meaning, she called out, 'Father Abraham, have pity on me; at the very least, speak to Barbara and see if she will put in a good word for me so I, too, can experience the meaning and joy of being in God's presence.'

"But Abraham replied, 'Have you forgotten that you in your lifetime had everything going for you and even more, and Barbara had nothing; and yet, you never extended yourself to her beyond a purely business relationship? And so Barbara is now comforted and you are in anguish. And besides all of this, between where you are now and where we are, there is a great gulf, which only God himself can bridge.'

"And the physician's wife said, 'Then I beg you, father, to somehow get the message across to many of my family and friends, lest they also end up as I have.'

"But Abraham said, 'They have their

churches and the Bible to read, let them see for themselves what is so obvious.'

"But she said, 'No, father Abraham, it just will not work! But if you could send someone to them from the dead, then they might wake up to the real meaning of life.'

"And Abraham said to her, 'If these family members and friends of yours are so dense and self-directed that they cannot see what is so blatantly obvious through what they profess to believe in their worship, and what they discuss with such fervor in their Bible studies, then neither will they be convinced if someone should rise from the dead.'"

THE LOST CUB SCOUT

"What man of you, having a hundred sheep, if he has lost one of them, does not leave the ninety-nine in the wilderness, and go after the one which is lost, until he

finds it? And when he has found it, he lays it on his shoulders, rejoicing. And when he comes home, he calls together his friends and his neighbors, saying to them, 'Rejoice with me, for I have found my sheep which was lost.'

"Just so, I tell you, there will be more joy in heaven over one sinner who repents than over ninety-nine righteous persons who need no repentance." (Luke 15:4-7)

"What man of you, having taken ten cub scouts on a camping trip into a wilderness area, if one of the youngsters wanders away and becomes lost, does not leave the nine by themselves at the campsite, and go after the child who is lost, until he finds him? And when he has found him, he picks him up in his arms, with tears of joy in his eyes. And when he gets back to camp, he calls together his troop, exclaiming with joyful relief, 'Look who I found! Let us celebrate tonight.'

"Just so, I tell you, there will be more joy in heaven over one sinner who repents, than over ninety-nine faithful believers who need no repentance."

"For it will be as when a man going on a journey called his servants and entrusted to them his property; to one he gave five talents, to another two, to another one, to each according to his ability.

"Then he went away. He who had received the five talents went at once and traded with them; and he made five talents more. So also, he who had the two talents made two talents more. But he who had received the one talent went and dug in the ground and hid his master's money.

"Now after a long time the master of those servants came and settled accounts with them. And he who had received the five talents came forward, bringing five talents more, saying, 'Master, you delivered to me five talents; here I have made five talents more.'

"His master said to him, 'Well done, good and faithful servant; you have been faithful over a little, I will set you over much; enter into the joy of your master.'

"And he also who had the two talents came forward, saying, 'Master, you delivered to me two talents; here I have made two talents more.'

"His master said to him, 'Well done, good and faithful servant; you have been faithful over a little, I will set you over much; enter into the joy of your master.'

"He also who had received the one talent came forward, saying, 'Master, I knew you to be a hard man, reaping where you did not sow, and gathering where you did not winnow; so I was afraid, and I went and hid your talent in the ground. Here you have what is yours.'

"But his master answered him, 'You wicked and slothful servant! You knew that I reap where I have not sowed, and gather where I have not winnowed? Then you ought to have invested my money with the bankers, and at my coming I should have received what was my own with interest. So take the talent from him, and give it to him who has the ten talents. For to every one who has will more be given, and he will have abundance; but from him who has not, even what he has will be taken away. And cast the worthless ser-

vant into the outer darkness; there men will weep and gnash their teeth.'" (Matthew 25:14-30)

"For the kingdom of heaven will be as when a private foundation made grants of seed money to three charitable agencies in the inner city. One agency received $35,000, another $20,000, and another $10,000. The directors of the first agency took their grant of $35,000 and set up a pilot program to aid youngsters suffering from child abuse. The directors of the second agency took their grant of $20,000 and funded a program to assist the housebound elderly. But the directors of the third agency took their grant of $10,000 and put the funds into a savings account.

"Now nine months later when the board of the private foundation was considering grants for the forthcoming year, they called in a representative of each of the recipient agencies to inquire as to the manner in which each had used the seed money. When the representative of the first agency had made his report, the president of the foundation replied, 'You have done well; count on another grant from us next year.'

"When the representative of the second agency had made his report, the president of the foundation said, 'You, too, have done a creditable job; count on another grant from us in the coming year.'

"But when the representative of the third agency had made his report, the president of the foundation said, 'What kind of initiative and vision is that?'

"And the agency's representative replied, 'We knew your foundation's reputation for being very demanding of its grant recipients and we did not wish to incur your disfavor by entering into an untested venture.'

"To which the president of the foundation replied, 'If you knew that we were willing to have vision enough to take risks with our funds, you should have done the same yourself. Those who hoard their treasure, because of the risk of loss, do nothing to liberate potential or to advance the common good. Do not ever expect to receive another grant from this foundation. Show this man to the door and let him lament his agency's financial plight and struggle to find funds elsewhere.'"

"The kingdom of heaven is like treasure hidden in a field, which a man found and covered up; then in his joy he goes and sells all that he has and buys that field."
(Matthew 13:44)

"The kingdom of heaven is like an oil find, which a man discovered on a certain piece of property and covered up; then in his joy he goes and raises all the funds he can and buys that piece of property."

THE FAULTY ATTITUDE

"But when the king came in to look at the guests, he saw there a man who had no wedding garment; and he said to him,

'Friend, how did you get in here without a wedding garment?' And he was speechless.

"Then the king said to the attendants, 'Bind him hand and foot, and cast him into the outer darkness; there men will weep and gnash their teeth.' For many are called, but few are chosen." (Matthew 22:11-14)

"When the chairman of the hospital's Charitable Gifts Committee began to evaluate the progress of their campaign, he came upon a committee member who was blatantly using this position only to enhance his social standing and business dealings in the community, and doing little for the hospital, except for consuming free food and drink at their gatherings. In observing this, he called the man into his office and said, 'I am going to be very candid. With your social-climbing attitude and behavior, how did you ever get on this committee?' And he was speechless.

"Then the chairman said to his secretary, after the man had departed, 'Send that man a letter informing him that his services are no longer needed. Hopefully, when the word gets around, people will see him for the phony status-seeker that he is; and then, when the invitations

104

to functions stop coming, he can sit at home and grit his teeth!' For many are invited to serve, but few are chosen."

THE WORLDLY INFIGHTING

"How can Satan cast out Satan? If a kingdom is divided against itself, that kingdom cannot stand. And if a house is divided against itself, that house will not be able to stand. And if Satan has risen up against himself and is divided, he cannot stand, but is coming to an end." (Mark 3:23-26)

"How can evil rid itself of evil? If a government is in anarchy, that government will fall. And if a husband and wife remain in a relationship of hate, that marriage will not be able to endure. And if organized crime engages in gangland wars and is divided, it cannot prevail, but will destroy itself."

"Truly, truly, I say to you, he who does not enter the sheepfold by the door but climbs in by another way, that man is a thief and a robber; but he who enters by the door is the shepherd of the sheep. To him the gatekeeper opens; the sheep hear his voice, and he calls his own sheep by name and leads them out. When he has brought out all his own, he goes before them, and the sheep follow him, for they know his voice. A stranger they will not follow, but they will flee from him, for they do not know the voice of strangers." (John 10:1-5)

"Truly, I say to you, he who does not go to the door of the classroom, but tries to entice children into his car when they are playing at recess, that man is no doubt a kidnapper or a child molester; but he who comes to the door of the classroom is the parent of the children. To him the teacher opens the door; the children hear his voice, and he calls his own by name and leads them out. When he has gathered all his children together, he walks with them to the car, and they tag along, for they recognize who he is. A stranger they will not follow, but they will flee from him, for they do not recognize his face."

THE WAYWARD DAUGHTER

"There was a man who had two sons; and the younger of them said to his father, 'Father, give me the share of property that falls to me.' And he divided his living between them.

"Not many days later, the younger son gathered all he had and took his journey into a far country, and there he squandered his property in loose living. And when he had spent everything, a great famine arose in that country, and he began to be in want. So he went and joined himself to one of the citizens of that country, who sent him into his fields to feed swine. And he would gladly have fed on the pods that the swine ate; and no one gave him anything.

"But when he came to himself he said, 'How many of my father's hired servants have bread enough and to spare, but I perish here with hunger! I will arise and go to my father, and I will say to him, "Father, I have sinned against heaven and before you; I am no longer worthy to be called your son; treat me as one of your hired servants."' And he arose and came to his father.

"But while he was yet at a distance, his father saw him and had compassion, and ran and embraced him and kissed him. And the son said to him, 'Father, I have sinned against heaven and before you; I am no longer worthy to be called your son.'

"But the father said to his servants, 'Bring quickly the best robe, and put it on him; and put a ring on his hand, and shoes on his feet; and bring the fatted calf and kill it, and let us eat and make merry; for this my son was dead, and is alive again; he was lost, and is found.' And they began to make merry.

"Now his elder son was in the field; and as he came and drew near to the house, he heard music and dancing. And he called one of the servants and asked what this meant.

"And he said to him, 'Your brother has come, and your father has killed the fatted calf, because he has received him safe and sound.'

"But he was angry and refused to go in. His father came out and entreated him, but he answered his father, 'Lo, these many years I have served you, and I never disobeyed your command; yet you never gave me a kid, that I might make merry with my friends. But when this son of yours came, who has devoured your living with harlots, you killed for him the fatted calf!'

"And he said to him, 'Son, you are always with me, and all that is mine is yours. It was fitting to make merry and be glad, for this your brother was dead, and is alive; he was lost, and is found.'"
(Luke 15:11-32)

"There was a man who had two daughters; and the younger of them said to him, 'Daddy, I have given this a lot of thought; I don't want to go to college. Please give me the money you have saved for my education so I can go to L.A., get an apartment, find a job, and just be on my own for a change.' And so her father, after much agonizing, gave her the money.

"Not many days later, the younger daughter gathered her things together and went to L.A., and over the next year she proceeded to squander her money on drugs, liquor, and fun times. And when her money was gone, she searched for any means to get by. So she moved in with a man, became pregnant, and he threw her out. She was unable to find work, her life was miserable, and she had nothing for herself.

"Then, considering her plight, she said to herself, 'How many of my father's employees are fairly well off and I'm living here in this dump?' And so she called her father and said to him, 'Daddy, I don't want you to say anything, just listen! I have really fouled up my life. I'm pregnant, I don't know what to do, and I am sure that you and Mom will feel like disowning me. I'm coming home on Friday. I thought maybe you could get me a job in the shipping department of your plant where nobody will know who I am; and I promise, I will get a room somewhere and keep away from the house and not be an embarrassment to you.' And she hung up the phone.

"Two days later, in absolute fear at what she was about to face, she got on a bus headed for home. As she was walking up the driveway, her parents saw her and had compassion, and ran and embraced her, kissing and hugging her ever so tightly. And she said, 'Oh, Daddy, I have really fouled up my life and disgraced you and Mom. How could you ever want me for your daughter?'

"But the father said to his wife, 'Let's get this kid in the house, get her cleaned up, and give her a good supper; and tomorrow, I want you to take her out and get her some new clothes. And I tell you what,' he said, turning to his daughter, 'You call your friends and tell them you're home and that your dad and mom are going to give you a big homecoming party next Saturday night. Honey, we all make mistakes, and your mom and I thought you were as good as dead, and that we might never see you again; and here you are, alive and well, and we just praise God for it!'

"Now her older sister was away at school, and by chance, she had called her aunt. And her aunt said to her, 'You will never believe what has happened; but I just got a call from your mother, and your sister has come home.' And she related the circumstances.

"Then her aunt said, 'Your mom and dad are going to throw a big homecoming party for your sister and her friends next Saturday night; I am sure you will want to be there!'

"Now the eldest daughter was angry. And she called her father and said to him, 'I just heard the news; and if you think I'm going to come home and go to a party for that tramp sister of mine, you're crazy. I just can't believe what you and Mom are doing. I don't shack up with guys, I've always been super good, I've never given you any big hassles; and yet, you never told me I could have a big party with my college friends. But when this darling daughter of yours comes home, who has wasted your money on drugs and partying, and done all sorts of immoral things, you make a big deal over her. I just can't believe you are doing this, Daddy. I think you are plain crazy and totally unfair!'

"And her father said to her, 'There is probably no way you will be able to understand and believe this now, but your mom and I love you more than we can possibly express, and always will, and there is nothing we wouldn't do for you. But just think for a moment about what has really happened in your mom's and my life. We had thought your sister to be lost to us forever, as good as dead; but now, she is home, alive and well, and the pain in our hearts is gone.'"